David James joined Premier League club Portsmouth F.C. in 2006. He is also a regular first choice goalkeeper for the England team, with 39 caps to his name. Before playing for Portsmouth David had spells with Manchester City, West Ham, Aston Villa, Liverpool and Watford.

Ping. My eyes are open. It's 7 o'clock in the morning on Saturday 17th May 2008.

2 Ah yes. Today is a big day.

Cup Final Day

by David James

Photos by Joe Pepler

GOAL!

Cup Final Day

by David James

Published by Ransom Publishing Ltd.

51 Southgate Street, Winchester, Hants.

SO23 9EH

www.ransom.co.uk

ISBN 978 184167 960 0

Cup Final Day (6 books) ISBN 978 184167 961 7

First published in 2008

Copyright © 2008 Ransom Publishing Ltd.

Photos by Joe Pepler.

All photographs copyright © 2008 Portsmouth Football Club.

Thanks to everyone at Portsmouth F.C. who gave invaluable help in developing this series.

A CIP catalogue record of this book is available from the British Library.

The moral rights of the author have been asserted.

Printed in the United Kingdom by HSW Print.

ChildLine
0800 1111

Need to talk?
Call ChildLine free, any time.

If you're deaf, or find it hard to hear or talk, textphone 0800 400 222. Or go to www.ransom.co.uk/forme

Portsmouth are playing Cardiff in

the F.A. Cup Final at Wembley.

And I'm in goal for Portsmouth.
No pressure, then.
The game starts in 8 hours.
And I am feeling nervous excitement.

The team stayed the night in a hotel near
Windsor. That's where the Queen lives.
I bet she's not feeling like I do right now.

Kick-off is at three o'clock.

Might as well catch up on some TV.

I'm just sitting here, waiting. There's nothing to think about. And there's everything to think about.

This is just a game, like any other game. We are playing Cardiff, and we can beat them

Hang on. It isn't just **a** game. It's **the** game. **The Cup Final**. My mind starts arguing with itself.

We go for a walk with our coach, Joe Jordan.
We do this before every away game.

And sure, I tell myself again,
this is just another away game ...

Everybody says you should enjoy F.A. Cup Final day. But it's only enjoyable if you win, I can tell you. I've lost twice before and I didn't enjoy it either time.

In 1996 Man U beat Liverpool in the Cup. I was playing for Liverpool. And in 2000 Chelsea beat Aston Villa. I was playing for Aston Villa.

Is this going to be third time lucky for me?

An hour and a quarter before kick-off. We arrive at the stadium. Wembley Stadium, in case I've forgotten.

You can feel the atmosphere. You can almost taste it. Suddenly it all feels very real.

Sure, I tell myself for the zillionth time,
this is just another away game ...

13

We wander out onto the pitch.
Time to soak up some of that atmosphere.

A lot of fans are already here.

We may look cool in our suits, but we are all so excited. We just want to get on with it now.

The ceremonies begin. Kathryn Jenkins and Lesley Garrett sing the national anthems.

It's all very nice but it makes us all feel the pressure even more.

I just want to start the game.
Then it'll be O.K.

17

It's time to go out onto the pitch.
This is better. It's nearly time for kick-off.

By the way, what a great stadium this is.
(Am I saying that just to have something
to think about?)

Now I'm O.K. This is my job.
I'm comfortable playing football.

Just concentrate and don't

make any big mistakes ...

A quarter of an hour into the game and I'm feeling a lot happier.

Remember, it's **just** a game of football ...

'No it isn't,'
says a little voice.

Twenty minutes in and our first real chance! Kanu beats their keeper and hits the post.

So close! Everybody groans and buries their heads in their hands.

Yes, even King Kanu! **25**

Yes! Gooaaal!

We're in the lead!

A great cross from John Utaka and Kanu just taps it in.

The fans go crazy. Thirty seven minutes gone and it's Portsmouth 1 Cardiff 0.

The ref. blows for half time.
We've kept that one-nil lead.

It's a good position to be in.

Harry Redknapp gives us his manager's half-time talk. He says change nothing. We've done well in the first half. Now we just have to keep going. Don't get silly, be sensible and keep the ball. But we have to watch their set pieces.

We're back out for the second half. We're doing O.K. We seem to be in control of the game.

Our defence is pretty solid. Everybody's playing a blinder.

I don't think Cardiff are going
to be able to break us down.

This is better. We're halfway through the second half now, and we're 1-0 up. Only twenty minutes to go.

It feels like we're in control. Cardiff are playing really well but we can do this.

As long as we don't make
any stupid mistakes.

The stadium speakers blare out.
Four minutes of added time start now.

Phew. Only four minutes to go. We're **that** close. 'You might do it' is going to turn into 'You've done it'...

Stop it! Concentrate on the game. We can still lose.

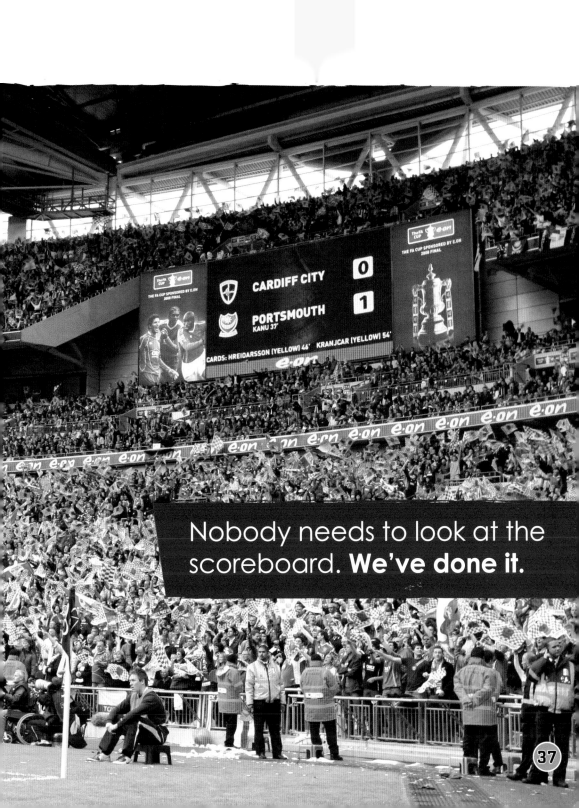

CARDIFF CITY 0

PORTSMOUTH 1
KANU 37'

CARDS: HREIDARSSON [YELLOW] 46' KRANJCAR [YELLOW] 54'

Nobody needs to look at the scoreboard. **We've done it.**

We have won the F.A. Cup!

I can't believe it. We have won the F.A. Cup!

It's going to take a while to sink in. But smiling seems like a great thing to do!

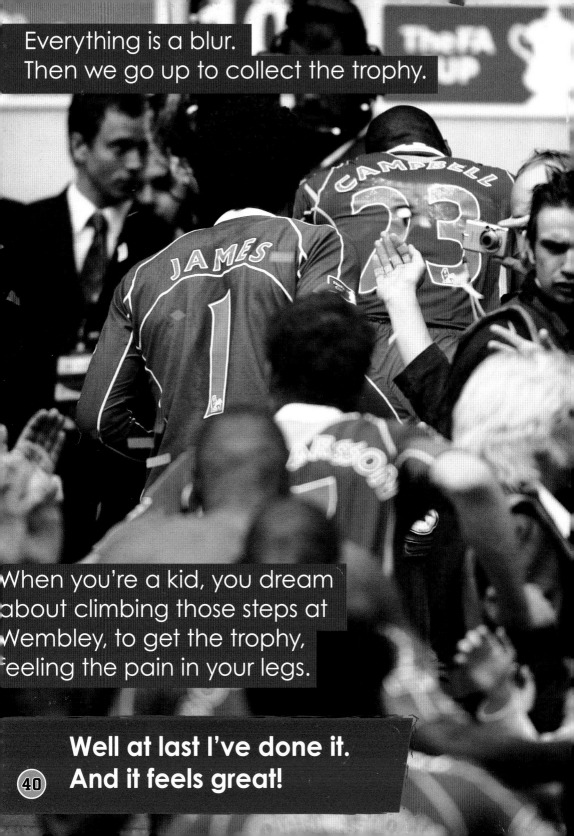

Everything is a blur.
Then we go up to collect the trophy.

When you're a kid, you dream
about climbing those steps at
Wembley, to get the trophy,
feeling the pain in your legs.

**Well at last I've done it.
And it feels great!**

It's a great moment.

And yet ...
You can see the Cup, you can see
your team mates. You can see the
score. You can see the fans.
But you still can't quite believe it.

It's time to enjoy this moment with our supporters.

I think we all feel the same.

For me, does winning the Cup make up for losing it twice before?

No, of course not. Losing hurts, really hurts. And winning is great. Right now, it feels like the greatest thing in the world. In the universe.

I hear Harry telling the BBC TV people that for him it's a dream come true.

It must be. He's waited 25 years for this. He so deserves it.

And, of course, celebrations carry on afterwards in the dressing room.

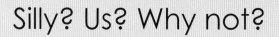

Silly? Us? Why not?

We have just won the Cup!

This is probably one for the photo album.

And then finally, after a long day, it was back to the hotel ...

Of course the Cup got to sit at the front.

One bus full of very tired
and very happy people.

And in the evening?
O.K., I admit it. We had a late night ...

The next day, back home in Portsmouth, 200,000 people came out to see us. Just fantastic!

FA CUP 2008

I don't know if my dream was to win the Cup, or to win the Cup and then share it with the fans.

Either way, we've done it.
And it feels good.

Really good.